66 Miles to Paradise

From Pomona Valley to the World

Gustavo Reyes Ramirez

a DSTL arts publication

66 Miles to Paradise

From Pomona Valley to the World

a DSTL Arts publication

Cover Design: Luis Antonio Pichardo

Original Cover Illustration: Gustavo Reyes Ramirez

Additional Illustration: Angel Fallon

Book Design: Luis Antonio Pichardo

ISBN: 978-1-946081-70-4

10 9 8 7 6 5 4 3 2 1

www.DSTLArts.org

DSTL
arts

Los Angeles, CA

Dedication

I'd like to thank my mama, my brother and my dad.
I've learned from all their qualities—the experience we've had.
I've found true friends are precious few—the brightest shiny stars.
For my True Familia. You all know who you are.
Gracias abuelit@s, TataraTuntun.
I find neighbors in all of you. Love thy neighbor through and through.
We all share Earth, our Mother, the skies and ocean blue.
All of my relations: We'll join together soon.
The bear of California. The condor shall fly with you.
The mighty Eagle Phoenix. We shall share skies of blue.
Thank you people of the Kizh. We've borrowed your great nation.
Yuhaviatam, Morongo, WE THE PEOPLE, all Creation.
¡No te rajes Durango! Huichol (Wixáritari), Odam—Mi Gente.
El Águila y el Nopal se miran en mi frente.
Arizona, Sonora Desert, the Río Colorado.
This mighty river will rush with cures, for water es sagrado.
Today I tell you, "Thank you," for wondering who I am.
I AM the love and peace of Christ Messiah. Together, yes we can.
Se grita, "¡Sí se puede!" Satyagraha sounds.
Please enjoy my music and laugh, for PEACE on EARTH abounds.
Journey with me to Heaven. It's there within your heart.
If you teach me as I teach you, together we shall start.
I present to you my life, like a tapestry unfurled.
Let us radiate love and peace and dignity,
       And we will heal the world

Table of Contents

Foreword i

I. Return of the Messiahs... 1

II. Innocence Lost 15

III. Welcome Home 27

IV. Pomona Shakespeare...47

V. Indigenous 55

VI. Dear Mama...69

VII. Chicano Haiku 77

VIII. The Border Crossed Us 93

IX. Last Section: The Beginning...105

Foreword

We begin by taking in a deep breath. We acknowledge All Creation. We honor the four sacred directions, the Sky and Mother Earth, as we give thanks to the Great Creative Spirit of all Life that connects us to one another as One. We thank Great Peacemaker, all healers and peacemakers. We ask for the courage and fortitude to become protectors of our Living Planet and creators of peace and dignity. We ask and receive Divine Guidance on our journey, so that we may become examples of courageous love. We uplift and support the Kizh/Tongva People—of Yagna (central Los Angeles), Toibingna (north Pomona), and of Torojoatngna (Claremont) at the Most Sacred "Indian Hill" Mesa, all in the Heart of Sacred Kizh Country,

...where my story begins.

I

Return of the Messiahs

If Tears Could Speak

If my tears could speak,
They would speak words of healing.
If my tears could act now, they would reach out and hold you.

Tears are alive.
They flow like waterfalls.
These tears cleanse our hearts.
They crystalize,
       And become diamonds.

          If my tears could speak, they would cry out for justice.
                    If they could turn back time,
                    They would say, "I love you."
                    If my tears could shout,
          They would shout from the rooftops.
                    If my tears could be captured,
          They would fight for our freedom.
                    If my tears could sing,
          They would wail your love song.

                    If my tears could speak.

                    If tears could tell a tale,
          They would rewrite our story.
                    If my tears could plead,
          They would beg your forgiveness.
                    If my tears could lie,
          They would say, "I don't need you."

If tears were forever,
We could create Heaven.
If my tears could yell,
They would cry out

your name

I'm Back Again: A Chicano Sonnet

One day I woke up with a broken heart
David told me about DSTL Arts
There'll be Angel and Tina—Abraham también
Luis Dreamed. Luis took action... Gracias a él
In East L.A. where we were born
Turn around the frown. Take away the scorn
I've looked for roses. But by thorns I've been scarred
Broken dreams on the Boulevard
David says, "They're gente with vision"
Come on little brother! Make that decision
Pick up the pen. Put down that sword
Get back to the lyrics, the artistic chord
There's no choice. You can come by train!
Good morning, Brave Mundo
                I'm back again

Avatar

Today I learn with addicts, lepers, and the thieves.
Ergo, I am emphatic. You who naysay should believe.
Castes and types of people; false hierarchies, we topple.
One addict to another; thieves become apostles.
You labeled me with scarlet—shunned me. Called me lunatic.
Though I'm God's staff like Moses, you say I'm worse than heretic.
Words don't seem to heal. But I grow wiser, yet I'm scarred.
Those who labeled me, I'll forgive: I'm A for Avatar.
Do you want to see me beaten—torn apart down to my core?
You succeeded. But I'm rising. I spread my wings and soar.
I love my neighbor; edify him; even called her "Angel".
Neighbors forget their God was spat on—homeless in a manger.
Christ knocks at your door, but you must unlock it.
The choice is yours to make, to heed lessons from a prophet.
Mother Earth and Sky; Ancestors; the Holy Spirit.
God's voice is speaking straight to you. Listen! You shall hear it.
The mayor, king, and all his men looked down at me with scorn,
But heavenly father chose me to live with this crown of thorns.
Citizens claim love for all, say they respect all of creation.
As they re-stone Mary Magdalene, they re-crucify Christ in
humiliation.
You build prisons and asylums. Indigenous build Freedom.
You call us vermin as we create y/our Garden of Eden.
Fake officials, presidents, dictators wanting more.
War mongers making money off the youngsters of the poor.
False pride we call hubris. Those who worship golden calves—
We teach you to be humble. A golden chance you have.

Yesterday we all were pirates. We awoke from the decks.

Today we are Messiahs. Gandhi-King sign on the X.

Hancock, Paul Revere, with Rosa Parks, now act as one.

Native Peacemaker, Christ and you take us to Kingdom Come.

Yet you still call me leper. As your masses applaud.

Though I've spoken in parables, it's clear you were a fraud.

You looked down with your arrogance. I do believe it's odd.

Your wealth buys camels and needles. What about Kingdom of God?

A wish is but a wish. A sin is but a sin.

Today I wash your eyes. You see! You let the goodness in.

When All Learn the Lesson: THERE IS NO LEAST OF THEE,

Then, and only then,

Will We Save Humanity

All I Want

*(Thanks to Maya Angelou, Jarvis Sams, Martin Luther King &
Jerry Hoffman)*

Broken and alone again.
Feel like I've lost a war.
I was born in paradise,
but all I want is more.

The fairy dust has blown away.
The magic carpet's gone.
Aladdin's magic lamp
was a smoke and mirrors con.

All I wanted was to change the world,
and peace throughout the land.
But I felt bitter betrayal
when I reached out for your hand.

But today I see a vision as the blind man starts to see.
They don't have to call you Moses. You don't have to part the sea.
He just may be a prophet as he claims he is no preacher.
"Knocking over tables takes strategy," says my social justice teacher.

The streets are dark and dangerous.
Another lonely night.
I look into the shadows.
I pray with all my might.

I look up to the heavens.

I may have lost my way.
There's a faint star left to guide me
as the night becomes the day.

Was a dream hijacked in Memphis?
Have you heard the caged birds sing?
Our children scream from cages.
They cry out, "Let freedom ring!"

And there's nothin' new under the sun,
though the faces may have changed.
As the star dies out in Baghdad,
the war is rearranged.

Let me be my brother's keeper.
Let me take a wounded knee.
Though we've looked up for the Savior,
      Chant together: **"It Starts With Me."**

The Greatest Prize

The faith of a mustard seed—be willing to believe
Listen to the Universe—messages to receive
Just sit still and meditate. The stress you will relieve
Sometimes they'll come like a quilt left up to you to weave

Listen to the songs, for music will abound
Some will be enlightening—some, oh so profound
Melodies and harmonies! Absorb all of the sound
Some will be made just for you—some for the whole world round

Look into the Heavens. You don't need a telescope
So fly among the stars. Ski the mightiest of slopes
Jewels and diamonds you will find, if your eyes intend for treasure
Emeralds are infinite—too much for you to measure

You'll learn many a lesson from the spirit of above
The greatest of the teachings—the greatest one is Love
And within you you'll find gold so precious. You'll find a surprise
Inside you will be Peace on Earth—this too, the Greatest Prize.

My Name is Bobby

I am Bobby and I'm addicted to justice. It is Peace for my People
    I crave
Give us freedom or give us death. I'll take this cause to the grave
Gandhi said, "It's do or die." This Causa is Sagrada
And if Jesus is the Prince of Peace, do Christians practice Satyagraha?
Rosary of Juana Estrada Chavez. Sacred Corazón
Holy Mary. Madre Nuestra. We dedicate esta canción
Images of Belfast strike. Sacred Heart bleeds for our Motherland
God has sent you His only son, who said, "My name is Bobby Sands"
Bombarded by flashes of Dublin, avalanche like a ton of bricks
I'm headed home to West Arlington. Pilgrimage on Route 66
"God please protect my child." Words every mother prays
The first shall be last. Bobby ended his fast—by dying on the 66th day
It takes long to die of hunger. I pray to God, "Please quench my thirst"
Of ten heroes who died in Her Majesty's Prison, our Bobby Sands
    was first
Now we march for all the Causas—from the Mountains to the Sea
As we weave movements together, sister chants "It starts with me"
God bless the San Patricios que tenemos en común
Virgencita and our Creator, Grant us Social Justice Soon
Who knew Irish and Our Indigenous would join—birds of a feather
Blessed are those who free the captives, as we win Causas together
Por 66 Causas Luchamos. Courage. Love. Peace. Dignity
Satyagraha, LA GRAN CAUSA. My Whole Being, I Give to Thee
Now we march 66 miles. It is but a grain of sand
We thrive through our pain and trials. We Shall reach the
    Promised Land.

Set Free

You can't fake it. You can't take it. The whole distanced world cringes.
The Superheroes have arrived. Messiahs come like ninjas.
The Revolution has begun. Not televised. No cable.
No satellite. Turn on the light. Be sure to heed this fable.
Let love rule. Your world in balance. Make sure that you're stable.
No wrath of God through pestilence. Don't slay like Cain & Abel.
The heavens rain purple & gold. I see it in your eyes.
The Kingdom in the mustard seed. Decode. Reveal the prize.
Not hieroglyphs, nor petroglyphs. It's black & white & simple.
The greatest one is love. One love will heal the crippled.
Discipline is growing, although they may entice.
Prayer joins with bold action, and we have Paradise.
Resuscitate like Lazarus—the blind will surely see.
Let the Christ shine from within you: The World Will be Set Free.

II

Innocence Lost

Save Me

I think I stepped on a landmine
In my nightmare.
Save me.
   Save me today.
My feet are underneath me,
But I'm sinking.
Save me.
   Save me today.
I cannot find my hands
To make sure my mouth is really speaking.
Save me.
   Save me today.
If I didn't have you all, I think I would have faded away, but I'm here.
And my face—my eyes and my lips are still working.
   And My Voice Still Speaks.

Unify

I thought I was a unifier, but what I did was protest.
Fancied myself a servant-leader. Put each other to the test.
I'd never cower, I wouldn't hide.
but what I did was just divide.

I feared the cops detested me. I was too much to handle.
And now I stand on sacred ground as I take off my sandals.
Forty days and forty nights—I listened, learned and prayed.
Today I am a newer man. I stand upright today.

We learn to give and learn to live, although we still will stumble.
I'm no better than you—you, no better than me. I aim to be
      forever humble.
You say "mosque". I say "church". He burns sage. She hears bells
      of steeples.
We need unifiers—human angels. Heart to heart. And we will save
      our people.

The Mexicano's ancestors, the first Americans.
But there's no you separate from I. There's we, like, "Yes we can.'"
We means you and I... loved former enemies and mended fences.
We healed our pain and we forgave. Gave up our differences.

As in a common shipwreck, we are birds of a feather.
Our differences make us alike. We can only do this together.
He was a peasant; you called them vermin. The king said, "Off with
      their heads."
But when both black and white men bleed, they bleed the color red.

18

I'd like to be your servant-leader. Maybe you can be mine.
And give respect to all nature. God, all the glory is thine.
You may say I'm just a dreamer,** but it's not "pie in the sky".
If there's just one thing to do: Muster all strength and Unify.
So I will lead and I will follow in my land of the brave.
And one by one—one at a time, this whole wide world, we'll save.

*Dolores Huerta

**John Lennon

That Lie

A lie that destroys
Is worse than killing.
For if they kill you
You don't feel anymore.
And you can rest.

But that lie that destroys
Kills your soul.
It shatters your heart.
And tears you apart
   Each moment,
     Day after day,
        Year after year
           ...an eternity

Esa Mentira

Una mentira que destruye
Es peor que matar.
Porque si te matan
Ya no sientes nada
Y puedes descansar.

Pero esa mentira que destruye
Te mata el alma.
Te parte el corazón.
Te destroza
   Cada momento,
    Día tras día,
       Año tras año
             ...una eternidad

White Lies

They call it a little white lie.
It grows into a black widow's web of deception.
Snow White's skin wasn't really white as snow.
I'm sure it was a shade of tan, with pink,
With a mask of makeup...
                    ...that   red   lipstick...

Maybe today she would be Coppertone.

White lies can grow.
White lives can grow.
White lines can grow.
Yes, that white lie can grow exponentially.

Before it explodes
Is the implosion.

Honesty is a good policy.
My honesty comes in rainbow.

Mad

I'm not crazy
I'm just lonely.
Isolated amongst the masses
I'm not crazy
I'm just hurt.
Shocked. Saddened. Betrayed.
Caught in desperation.

I don't think I'm crazy
Though you called me "lunatic".
–Just deeply disappointed
Disturbed by your callousness
Afraid for our futures.

Just outside of the hospital–the mental hospital–grows a Sycamore.
"Shavar", in the name of the local Kizh / Tongva tribe. So I tell
the shrink (who I call "Dr. Feelgood") to protect the Sacred
Shavar right outside the window. "It's sacred, and, you know,
the greenhouse effect." The doctor looks at me as if I'm
"crazy" even by mental hospital standards. "You're
undermedicated."
"He's misdiagnosed. More likely, Schitzo-effectve. Send him to
unit four."

I'm afraid for our future,
When no one seems to listen.

As I ask to heal one another.
How can you remain so calm as our beautiful world catches fire?

And are you really sane,
or has the entire world
  gone
      Mad
          ???

III
Welcome Home

On Sunset

I was born on Brooklyn Avenue, right next door to East L.A.
Just east of Sunset Boulevard, where the Hollywood boys play.

Now, I've had my share of heartache... And I've felt my share of pain.
Still, I try and keep my head up, though I fake and I may feign.

Stuck inside another rehab. This used to be a grand hotel.
They tried to build another Hollywood. It's the flashy gates of hell.

They say palm trees line the boulevard. They say the streets are
      paved with gold.
But the streets are tough in SoCal. It's where hustlers must be bold.

Welcome to Southern California. And the city of L.A.
Meaner than your mama told ya'. This angel city knows my name.

You can reach your dreams on Sunset. Most just watch their
      dreams explode.
You're surrounded by all the people. But you're on that lonely road.

With a pitstop in Pomona, from the mountains to the sea.
Let condors fly above Route 66. And that eagle will fly free.

Why do I feel like I'm in prison? It's called rehabilitation.
Some say it's the house of pain. But I call it transformation.

They changed my street to Cesar Chavez, underneath the skies of blue.
Not too far from Martin Luther King.
            Join me and make that dream come true

Freedom

I thought I was the only soul that God would never save
But the people of the 12 steps said I was never born a slave
I was captive in a prison. I was shackled up in chains
But these bars were invisible, for my shackles were my pain
Some are chained up by the bottle. Others, shackled to the pipe
It started as an illusion. I got lost in all the hype
Back when I was just a lad, I had a deep affliction
Red flags were waving, needed saving, beginnings of addiction
Later I was flyin' high. A great position. Great career
But what I didn't know did hurt me—for I was to live my greatest fear
I switched from scotch to brandy, then from whiskey, rum and Jack
You may drink until you black out, or may switch from Coke to crack
One day in Pomona Valley, I got popped for substances
So I walked into the Triangle Club to change my circumstances
I felt a touch of freedom. But it slipped right through my hands
No willingness, no open mind. I didn't understand
I wanted to be Superman. I was not quite Clark Kent
Without the pipe or bottle, I was nervous and discontent
Now I had another challenge. As my problems multiplied
Without the social lubricant. Kamikaze suicide
So one day I got a sponsor and I poured out my whole heart
So my spirit guide then told me, "You are off to a great start"
I admitted I was powerless. I began to do step one
I admitted total failure, then freedom began to come
Now I became teachable 'cause I was kicked straight to the curb
My way didn't work so I became humble and began to serve
We may not always get along but I know you're one of me

I may not do this perfectly. Because of your love, I am free
Now today we're at the Write Meeting. Welcome to these steps
       to freedom
We are rebellious addicts who have come into the kingdom
Today I learn a lesson. It took a life for me to see
We who lived our lives in slavery—today we're given liberty.

The First Supper

It's another day today. It's extremely tough.

Another relapse Thursday. I'll say, "Enough's enough."

Damn. This feeling's horrible. It's truly for the birds.

How many times will I sing this song? It's time to change the words.

Sponsor's shocked and a bit upset. He looks at me dismayed.

"What happened this time, Gus?" On that fateful day.

I chose to drink. I chose to use. A tightrope on these fences.

Now it's time to man up and face the consequences.

When we write the story of my life, what will the people say?

They say I'm the one who counts. I'm sober here today.

Today I sing a new song. Los pericos fly above.

The canary in the coal mine. Song of the mourning dove.

Why do we mourn this new day? The sun rises in the east.

It's not the last—it's the first supper. So prepare to make this feast.

The dawn of faith. The Sabbath breaks. The horizon shines ahead.

Put down poison. Pick up the host. It's time to break the bread.

The Messenger

When anyone, anywhere reaches out in desperation
There is a fellowship that wrote a declaration
I felt that I was dying. Amongst the crowd I was alone
Inside I was crying. I was bruised down to the bone
A social justice warrior. Fighting a lost cause
Fighting for equal justice, but I broke all of the laws
Thought I'd fight like Malcolm X or maybe Martin Luther King
Trying to find my way to Heaven. Chased impossible dreams
I even fought against myself—so why on Earth would you care?
The quote says, "I want the hand of AA always to be there"
So you opened up your heart. You reached out your hand
I had searched the seven seas and all throughout the land
I was like a passenger in a shipwreck, stranded on an isle
But, see, you were shipwrecked too, and blessed me with a smile
I saw only doom and gloom. I was at the end of my rope
You carried a message of experience, strength and hope
I never thought someone could like me, 'cause I did not love myself
You told me, "You are one of us." You showed me my inner wealth
I'm not a knight in shining armor. I'm not Martin Luther King
I'm just an alcoholic, but now I hear freedom ring
A new freedom, a new happiness. I learned of the promises
I embarked on a new beginning. Welcome to my genesis
I may not be Superman, flying through the sky
But I walk with dignity. And I hold my head up high
God works a string of miracles. My dreams are coming true
If God can save a wretch like me, this can also work for you
Before I had no lifeboat. I was a shipwrecked passenger

Now I bring you good news, for I am
the Messenger

The Winds of Change

Elder sensei taught me lessons. Said the winds of change will blow.
Plant your roots deep in the soil and be prepared to grow.
Like a bamboo in the garden, whose roots you cannot see.
No one can judge my will to change, as I know change starts with me.
Half measures avail us nothing. Standing stagnant gives us nil.
Chinese proverb teaches to take those steps. No one grows while
　　　standing still.
A Colorado spirit guide told me, "Growth starts when you do
　　　not boast."
The wolf that you help grow stronger is the wolf that you feed
　　　the most.
So feed your heart with courage. Don't feed your mind no trash.
When you clean your house, you will surely rise like a phoenix from
　　　the ash.
Don't you cower down from heroic action—background or front
　　　line, just don't hide.
We march on. We're the peaceful warriors. Let the brave heart be
　　　your guide.
Nana Abuelita taught me. Gramma glimmered as she grew old.
Your bright aura shines through your inner light as your action
　　　grows more bold.
I learned a secret in this fellowship—self talk helps keep me free.
They may judge me harshly. Call me insane. As I grow, I talk to me.
So I'm conversing with myself today, and I'm dancing in the rain.
Though I hear that suffering's optional, my coach teaches that
　　　growth takes pain.
But today though I look, I cannot feel hope. I've seen success but

the light is gone.

If this is growth, then I've been betrayed, and forsaken is my song.

See, I'm glad you came here, brother. Sister, you are one of me.

I am one of you—don't deny. Know the truth shall set you free.

It's amazing grace. Please accept embrace. See, our love will let
    you be.

Though this morn I lost the sunshine—seemed a lost soul in the night.

But we see your soul and we love your heart as you grow into the light.

So go onward, mis hermanos. We go forward, quick or slow.

When you fall: Fall forward. When you step: Step onward. "We
    got you" as you grow.

My Own Alcatraz

I was poor among the masses. I was longing to breathe free
Till a fellow told me, 'Son, come and follow me'
Some call it "Freedom", some "Independence", some call it "Liberty"
All I know is I was blind, but now my eyes can see
They said there would be promises. New Freedom and Happiness
Told me if you take these steps, you will fill that emptiness
See, I never been to Folsom, though I feel stories the prisoner has
Never been to Soledad, but I've been in my own Alcatraz
See, "soledad" means lonely—Spanish for a broken heart
They break my corazón like the ocean Moses parts
Now I'm back home and I wander. You may call it Tale of Woe
I don't expect a hero's welcome, and it's loneliness I know
When I came, I was a captive in the prison of my mind
Just Ask, Knock, Open, & Walk—then it's Freedom you
         shall find
No, I might not be a millionaire, but like an eagle I am free
Free to fly above the valleys, from the mountains to the sea
I take a step on the pilgrimage, we triumph through the arch
I walk the walk of dignity, and march the sober march
And we scale the Rocky Mountains with the courage of a ram
Like that Mountain Top in Montgomery. As Rosa marched in
         Birmingham
Today Tecumseh's vision meets the likes of Paul Revere
Though we sing the songs of freedom, the Red Road crossed
         Trails of Tears
Freedom one day at a time. You shall be freed from your past
We can hear that Ring of Freedom. We can breathe. We're free at last

Eureka

Still nervous. Still restless. Uncomfortable in my skin
I fought hard for success. I've tried so hard to win
I kept on trudging forward. But then I'd fall right back
I'd move along the sober road then fall right off the track
Today I'm substance-free. Naysayers ask a question
Just when I have my head up, the critics always mention
They bring up all the monsters. Acknowledge all the flaws
I'm more than criticisms. I am not your lost cause
I'm bamboo in the orient that shoots into the sky
I'm condor in the Andes soaring through the skies so high
With the vision of a hawk, I see you with my heart
To those who claim I've lost, I say, "This is but the start"
The beginning of a journey, navigating through the strife
Like the captain of a ship, sailing on this boat called Life
We move forward through the maze. Don't get stuck in winding
        hallways
Listen to the sound of nature. Zenzontle echoing "Tiahui"
Move onward. Yes, move forward. Open up to understand
Though you've looked elsewhere for paradise, sacred ground is
        where you stand
You have traveled through horizons, to lands both far and near
You can finally shout, "Eureka!" You have found it. You are here.

Fireworks to a Pyromaniac

Fireworks to a pyromaniac
Shooting stars on a night so black
From the beaches to the desert, palm trees hide what's tragic
Hollywood to Vegas, streets are lined with magic
Obsession with the alchemy, the magician is a fraud
Wise man emerged: "Where do you stand with your God?"
The second hand is ticking. I'm afraid it'll be too late
Angel and demon tug at me. The temptation is so great
The master of seduction, I want to flee just as I stay
Comes in the form of blissful angels, even as I pray
Father please forgive them, for the grace belongs to you
How can God forgive me? I know exactly what I do
When I was but a child—innocent and childish ways
Now that my eyes have opened, I see the end of days
Footprints in the sand, till I give in to addiction
Good intentions pave the road straight to dereliction
God never promised roses without cuts and pain from thorns
Time's right to take the bull and ram both by the horns
Smoke and shadows vaporize. Time to end the contradiction
The fire of the laser. I must manifest the mission
I survive seven tsunamis as the walls come tumbling down
I surrender to your kingdom. I finally give you my crown
You say "crown". I say "corona", as God lifts this malady
Now I build a new foundation based on TRUTH
                                    as we're set free

Alluring

Fatal. Cunning. Shocking & Alluring
Just one more dance. I'll take that chance. This hell—it is enduring
Seems like Lucky Charms but it's kryptonite
It's the thief that breaks in through the night

Those Laser lights beam through your eyes. You see with such
precision
Master superpowers in the midnight hours, till you cry for an
exorcism
How can it feel good for your soul, yet be worse than a heart attack?
I was seeing the lights of paradise till everything went black

Snow White's magic fairy dust. Infinite Magic crystals
But dangerous like lightning. More deadly than a pistol
The hero of the story. My savior, Heroin
You caused me deepest suffering, yet I'd return again
Kept coming back for more. Could not control my brain
Satan's got his entire crew, led by liquor & cocaine

Ashes to ashes, dust to dust. This gold of fools has turned to rust
I had searched the heavens for ecstasy. It betrayed and broke
my trust
The angel dust is gone. The genie disappeared
Now I'm walking on the tightrope looking for angels to appear

Won't take another toke. I'm broken & I'm broke
My dreams went straight through rolled-up bills as they went up
in smoke

I've been to jails & institutions as death touched me all too close
And now it's your turn to live this tale. No death by overdose

Now there's Part Two, but it's up to you. Don't end up in that grave
Rock bottom often has a deeper trap so take our hand that saves
Sweet chariot can take you home but home is out and up
We are the Recovery Band of Angels. And you are safe with us
This tale is everlasting. These are bonds that do not sever
Don't betray yourself. Join our mission. Our love lasts forever.

From Pomona to Tokyo

    Block 'em.

        Shock 'em.

The screams inside. Just bust it out.

Lift it. Encrypt it. False Confessions lurk about.

Wheelin'. Dealin'. From Pomona to Tokyo.

Venice Blvd. MLK. We blast off.

To cruise so slow.

Holt Blvd. Don't cross that yard, for here we don't go solo.

Never saw a hustler with a Master's in Experience.

Welcome international, just when you thought you were makin' sense.

Diamonds. Platinum. Got a torch. Melt 'em like plastic.

Around the world in 90 sec's—we'll go intergalactic.

Never witnessed rhymes like these.

Gangster punk'll have you on your knees.

Not really a gangster—too infinite to measure.

Destroying crystals of cocaine. Unlock the greatest treasure.

You may call me "tweaker" as I blow away your meth.

From the proud and to the meeker—you're Messiah. I'm the breath.

Didn't graduate from Yale.

Read the letter from that jail.

Taught me lessons. Thought I missed 'em.

Hypothesize that I'm a fool. I teach the crowds at Princeton.

Millionaires. Billionaires. Corporate bosses of the hood.

You can call me fiend. I'm a calculating Robin Hood.

Won't take that toke. Ain't no joke. You feel that I'm a kidder.

You love me on that Instagram and follow me on Twitter.

Though you're upside-down, don't cower down into dismay.

44

Turn it up. That's wassup. Now break it up. See master. Disobey.
I see demons in the shadows—or is that the mighty stalker?
Prostitutes. Addicts rule. The capital of street walkers.
Father, please forgive them for they know not what they do.
In my hood, brown vs. brown. Let's unite the Red & Blue.
Stick to the script. Don't contradict. Call us infamous tweakers.
Technicality. Reality. We're the Truest of the Seekers.
Bhagavad Gita. Kabbalah. I add the Kama Sutra.
When you think it's Armageddon,   **it's the Beginning of the Future**

IV

Pomona Shakespeare

Chicano Sonnet: I Am

I am Mexica Quetzalpapalotle.
You say, "Be careful. Do not rock the boat."

I am the lightning and the sound of thunder.
Yet do not want to end up six feet under.

I know we're all destined to turn to dust,
With you, I'll change the world. Do this, I must.

I must take risks ever so calculated.
I'm loved by many. Also, I am hated.

I show you many ways that I transform.
Just like an ocean dances in the storm.

I am the Phoenix dancing in the fire,
To songs of angels singing in the choir.

I am the real one. I don't mean to boast.
Pueblo!   Tiahui!   Onward from coast to coast.

Sonnet to Save the World

I woke up to the breaking of my heart.
I was so sad, then shifted on a dime.
I went to Conchas and began to rhyme.
With others joined, we're off to a great start.

"The start of what?" people began to ask.
This day's a new beginning for the world.
But doom and gloom on the news, I have heard.
To save the planet, this is our great task.

The chosen generation, that is us.
A present and responsibility.
A sacred gift from God to you and me.
We must take action and not just discuss.

Our curse and blessing, this is for the brave.
Let's join together and this world we'll save.

Sonnet for the Addict

I changed when I found out that time was ripe.
I put away the bottle and the pipe.

I could no longer wait until tomorrow.
I broke so many hearts and caused much sorrow.

I'm often arrogant, and sometimes meeker.
You call me drug addict. They call me tweaker.

Loaded with the "paizas". Pues, yo hablo.
Hablo español con Dios y diablo.

The devil tried to put me in the hole.
Into the grave—was tryin' to take my soul.

At the mental hospital, Canyon Ridge.
I used to bury all, then built a bridge.

Now God has won! My life, I've started over.
This sonnet ends. I live life clean and sober.

Pomona Proud: A Gay Pride Sonnet

They promised me that I could reach the moon.
I reached for the stars one day late in June.

I wanted someone close—here by my side.
Someone who's not afraid to show their pride.

The rainbow shines as I am in the ark.
Like Noah felt as he had left the dark.

We're in this ark destined for foreign lands.
To show the world our pride—gay, straight, bi, trans.

But I know my roots. Started in Cali.
So my gay pride promotes Pomona Valley.

I grew up alone. Many nights I cried.
Now we're here together. We show our pride.

We won't be silent. We will yell out loud.
At the new pride center: Pomona proud.

V

Indigenous

WATCH US

Part I

The shrink* yelled, straight out, "You are bipolar! You're so
nervous you can't even work at Jack in the Box,
much less help students from Pomona win the Nobel Peace Prize."
Watch Me.
Watch Us as we rise like that Phoenix from the burning flames.
See, Resurrection is from where I came.
Staff of Creator is my God-given name.
And explosive like butane is the name of my game.
The impact on this world—it'll never be the same.
Together we're unstoppable like a high-speed train.
What makes us invincible is that we thrived through the pain.
Wanted us out. Through your doubt, though you shout with disdain.
You can't measure our hearts. Can't disable my brain.
You can shoot   as it suits.   You kick me with your boots.
It's insane. Though you feign. Your false reign is insane.
So don't blame   us or tame   or extinguish our flame.
You may think this Phoenix Dies   but I Rise   through the Skies.
I know of your lies,
so retreat from where you came.
Revive.   Rebirth.   Reawaken our name.
We will win at this game.   Your disdain   is in vain.
So Watch Me, Watch US as you envy our Fame.
This Victory's Ours As Crowds Stand to Acclaim.
There's no shame   as you praise   Our Victorious Flame.

You thought that your words would stop us forever?
Don't cry me a river.
My skin is of Bronze. Ancestors' hair is of Silver.

She's 14 and they say she's never gonna graduate from high
school, and she doesn't have a chance in hell to go to college.
Watch Her.

The teacher said, "JC—he'll never amount to anything. He's only
12, and he's gonna be at the wrong place at the wrong time, and
he's never gonna live to see 18."
Watch Him.
Watch Us–
As my head's underwater and I gasp for air.
Do you call him crazy as he pulls out his hair?
For He is in You and You are in Me. We find inspiration—I don't
know from where.
It must have been God 'cause no one else was there.
We used to sit like prey in a lion's lair.
But there's no use for self-pity. We all have a cross to bear.
Watch us as we help each other when no one seems to care.
As we work for justice in a world that's not fair,
As we rise from the ashes of our despair.
See, when the world cried "Violence" Dr. King was there.
As we act with courage when all others are too scared.

Part II

WATCH.

Not just me, see it's us,

And we're watchin' them Back.
Better than watching, We ACT.

...Watch yourself
'Cause We See
(the Whole World is Watching!)
And we've seen
See, we have seen the Glory of the comin' of the...

You'll never amount to what?
I saw little J.C. today.
He told me:
I'm not J.C.
My name is Joaquín Cuauhtémoc.
Guess what? I made it. And as I made it to 18, I can make it to 19,
and 20, and 30...   and 40...
WATCH ME.
WATCH US.
For when my wings were broken on the curb, you left.
This Phoenix is risen from the ashes of your contempt.
Not a thug soldier.
Now that I'm older,
I join with the Condor.
I am the Eagle Phoenix.

We are the dynasty,
Building the legacy.
Down with destruction.
Stop the corruption.
Said, We are the dynasty,
Building the Legacy.
No more hypocrisy.
Fulfill The Prophecy.

Don't just watch me. Unite! And Together We Fly.
...and together the Condor, the Eagle, the Phoenix Unite and Fly
High in the Sky.

The legend of the Phoenix has Transformed in the Fire into the
Prophecy of the Eagle & the Condor.
WE JOIN. WE RISE.

*name omitted to protect the guilty

We the People

They taught me not about the deergrass,
But my tío gathered Quelite.
Elders taught about hierbas,
Y Mamá usa el metate.
And I learned about the hawk on high,
As I longed for Eagle to fly.
Fertile ancestors' sisters, frijol,
As my dream echoed, "Huichol!"
Though I thought it was a dove,
Falcon, 'quiliqui', above...
El Águila cantó,
As my corazón se partió.
Genocide still plagues the children.
Wampanoag saved the "pilgrim".
To Europe they were endemic.
They call it victory—we say pandemic.
Hiawatha, the Five Nations,
Built USA creation.
Twisted history to distortions—
Plague of Biblical proportions.
I see mark of the beast,
Yet I eat your thanksgiving feast.
And you say to change my attitude.
I muster strength, love, faith and gratitude,
Though our knowledge was killed by massacres.
I feel millions of ghosts of Gatherers.
Gathered to pray, and, at once, dance.

Yet you killed with gun and lance.

Our common souls did not break.

You killed your own heroines at the stake.

We could have made true friends and learned—

Yet King Cuauhtémoc's feet, you burned.

Ya, de México venimos,

A mejorar los Estados Unidos.

Grandfather is rising tall.

Mamá prepares the nopal.

Tata enciende el copal.

They tell me to give my best to all.

Este nopal está en mi frente.

"We the People" son mi gente.

The Bamboo and the Pilgrimage

Odam for We the People.

The pine trees are our steeple.

Collided with the Nahuatl in the Sierra of Durango.

Sanctuary of Cahuilla. The Rez is called Morongo.

Serrano are Yuhaviatam. The People of the Pines.

Long ago we were one people. Close to the dawn of time.

The bamboo and the pilgrimage.

The Huichol are our heritage.

White power. The supremacists

Don't have to be our nemesis.

Mi tatarabuela—when she was very young—

You killed the tribe and took her language. You replaced her tongue.

The cactus and the grass. The moon and stars at night.

Jupiter and Mars. The sun that shines so bright.

We've been here for so long. We will not fade away.

We didn't cross the borders. It's right here we will stay.

Indian Summer

As a brave it is my duty. I'll search high and low and far.
I'll move mountains for our people. On the backdrop are the stars.
In the supper of millennia, I give you bread. Please break it.
Creator shines upon us. Pray to Spirit that's so sacred.
You call this Indian Summer. We call it Winds of Change.
Although the planets shift, the stars don't rearrange.
And Native meditation. The Toltec tales of old—
You call it the way. We call it the Red Road.
The hawk gives you a sign. On your path, it drops a feather.
We're in the ship that's sinking. We must save the Earth together.
A small window of time. The time to break the curse.
Join us in this endeavor. To heal the universe.

Indian Country

I.

People say to me I wasn't raised on the rez.
I was born en la selva de Los Ángeles,

Raised in the jungle of Pomona.

But I know only Indian Country.
"Were you born on the rez?" you ask.

I was born in Yagna, by the river.
In the shadow. Of the spirit. Of the Shavar.

"Tildío! Tildío! Tildío!" The killdeer asks this question:
"When you speak to the birds,
 Do the birds sing back to you?"
When I talk with the parrots,
The wild parrots dance for me.
Do you dance with the birds?
With the bear?

Do you howl with the wolves?

You ask me, "Where were you born?"
I ask, "How do you live?"

You say I'm not a real indian
Because my tatarabuelo was from Spain.

I say I'm truly Indigenous, 'cause

My mother told me to Aim
To Aim high
To Aim forever

Forever AIM.

Yes, I know only Indian Country.
I was born just south of Yuhaviatam land.
Yuhaviatam—the People of the Pines.
I was raised just south of Mt. Baldy,
In Toibignga.

All I know of are lands that were stolen.
But you recovered them!
They're reclaimed by you!
So all I know of is Indian Country:
California. Colorado. Canada.
New York. Sonora Desert. Durango.
Machu Picchu. Brazil: The Amazon!
Puerto Rico.
Cuba.
The Turtle Islands.
Indian Country.

All I ever see
Is Indian Country.

So they ask me where I was raised.
I'itoi tells me the question is, "Have you met your spirit guide?"
"In your sleep, do you fly through the eyes of the dreamcatcher?"

I ask, "Do you sleep awake?"
As you sleep, do you awaken to the great truth?

The great truth that your mother is dying.
You've got to act like your mother is on fire.

She is.

II.
Mother Earth

And as you kill your mother,

      as the wolf mother howls that last gasping cry to the moon.
      as the white man in red skin,
      as the brown man in white robes...

When the world finally finds out that
      you can't eat money.
      you cannot drink oil.

When the Hopi elder says:
      "This is the hour,
      this is the minute,
      this is the second..."

When the condor and the eagle and the prophecy seem to burn out.

As the world breathes its last dying breath,
Will your Mother rise up and call out
      your
         name

            ?

VI

Dear Mama

Here. Con Mi Madre

She Who Stands... O Tonantzin

O Guadalupe!

Mother's greatest gift

We all come from Mother Earth

HONOR OUR MOTHER.

Le Coeur de la Mer

The Heart of my Mother. Le Coeur de la Mer
When all others tire, there's one who still cares
The Great One taught us to "Love one another"
But there's one whose love is like no other
The Heart of the Ocean. Corazón del Mar
She Lights Up When She Smiles from Near or from Far
While we may all learn lessons from teachings of our fathers
If some mothers reach Sainthood, my Mom would walk on water
Enseñanzas de mi Madre: Amor, Respeto y Paz
Perdone mis ofensas
Eres Mujer Capáz
Mi primera palabra—Our First Love is Mama
God reminds de tu Milagro en la Estrella de la Mañana
The Morning Star, Ese Lucero, Rainbows and Shooting Stars
I always make a wish—no matter where you are
You taught me faith and gratitude—taught me to face my fear
On days that you seem far away, I always hold you near
This is why, when others may be smart, charming or clever
   A Mother Shines Above Us All
       Mama's Love is Forever

My Mama Tells Me

My Mama tells me, "Sí se puede"
As some say, "Yes we can"
"Begin with the end in mind"
"Don't ever fail to plan"
But one day in the early morn
or was it 15 long hard year?s
My plans and dreams were broken & I couldn't hold back tears
I tried harder by myself, but couldn't take it any longer
Voz de mi Tía Elisa: "Together we are stronger"
Others said I'll never make it
My mom said I can
I admitted total failure and reached out for your hand
It was after that moment that I saw the morning dew
I found God does work miracles
God Comes to Me Through You

Mi Mamá Me Dice

Mi Mamá me dice, "Sí se puede."

Unos dicen, "Yes we can."

"Empiece con el final en mente."

"Nunca dejes de planear."

Pero un día por la madrugada, o quizás 15 largos años,

No pude contener mis lágrimas, y mis sueños fueron quebrados.

Traté de hacerlo solo pero ya no aguanté.

Voz de mi tía Elisa, "Juntos Somos Más Fuertes." Esto escuché.

Unos dicen que yo no lo lograré. Mi mamá dice que sí.

Yo extendí mi mano. Fracaso admití.

Fue después de ese momento que el rocío yo miré.

Me dí cuenta que Dios sí hace milagros. Me alcanza a través de Usted.

Lo que eres es instrumento de la paz.

Milagros pasan cuando menos esperas.

VII
Chicano Haiku

El Gran Shavar Tree

We need a new style of art

East meets Our Gente

Chicano Haiku

Indigenous Goes Worldwide

Únete Pueblo

We destroy our pond

What is the sound of water?

No one's left to hear

Nagasaki cries

I see Hiroshima skies

Fukushima dies

Carmen Masaki

La de mi Abuelito

Tokyo esta'qui

Lands of the Southwest

El Norte de México

Our People. Odam.

A Dream or Vision?

Bamboo Rises to the Sun

Huichol in the East

Creator weaves webs

Let's weave movements together

Weave Movements of Love

¿Donde 'stá La Voz?

El Sonido de Agua

No Quedó Nadie

Agua Es Vida

Protect Water & Our Earth

Mni Wiconi

Stewards of Nature

Make This Land Native Again

Say, "INDIGENOUS"

Act with Hope and Faith

The greatest of these is Love

Love can Save the world

World greed addiction

Break the addiction cycle

Give hope to the world

VIII

The Border Crossed Us

The Same Moon

This sávila will heal your wounds... and all the secrets of the pines
From Durango to Morongo. La Misma Luna shines
They tried to destroy the knowledge our People took great pains
       to learn
They ravaged gold like vultures. The codexes, they burned
The mockingbird lands on el mesquite, then through the skies this
       bird flies free
As Indian trails wind through mountains, that sacred mountain
       holds the key
Creator sends another rainbow. Brand new Covenant for us to keep
Let's promise that the bears will flourish, though today the willows weep
500 years of pillage. But they could not take my soul
They killed the grizzlies, wolves, eagles, condors... The sacred jade,
       they stole
Mama lives in California. Left chirimoyas in Montoros
Farewell sparrowhawks and orioles. Onto other arroyos
We did not realize our golden treasure, la urraca in the spring
They all frolicked in the garden where that jaybird loved to sing
Where shall the mourning dove coo? Where will the lizards roam?
It may not mean that much to you, but you haven't lost your home
The news didn't film our paradise. The world didn't mourn the cost
Silent tears drop on this trail... Cry of the forest, "Paradise lost."
Cucurrucú paloma. Do not cry for me
Though I'm in "El Otro Lado", La misma Luna, I can see
Oh say, we see el mismo cielo from Enero to December
When the sight's La Misma Luna,
              The moon and the stars remember

La Misma Luna

Los secretos de los pinos sanarán tus heridas
Desde Durango hasta Morongo, La misma luna brilla
Memorias. Madre mía. Dejamos en la Sierra Madre
Este hoyo en mi alma. Las heridas que se abren
Trataron de destruir la sabiduría que nuestro pueblo aprendió
Como auras, robaron oro. Códices sagrados, Cortez quemó
El zenzontle llega al mezquite. Mamá apunta al agave
Caminos indios corren por los cerros. En la Montaña está la llave
Creador manda a un arcoiris. Promesa nueva hay que honrar
Prometemos que los osos prosperen, aunque se escucha a el
      sauz llorar
500 años de raptar, pero mi alma no mataron
Mataron a los osos, lobos, águila y condor... Robaron el jade más
      sagrado
Mamá vive en California. Dejó chirimoyas de Montoros
Adiós quiliquis. Adiós gorriones. Encontraremos otros arroyos
Recordaré el paraíso donde esa urraca podía jugar
En el jardín jugaban todos... el zenzontle se oía cantar
No llores por mí, paloma. Pajarillos ya están tristes
Quizás a tí no te duele esto, pero tu hogar, no la perdiste
Miramos todo un tesoro. Yo miro diamantes—Tú miras lodo
Estas lágrimas de cristal... Criaturas lindas perdieron todo
La tele no filmó este paraíso. El mundo no lloró
Lágrimas silenciosas en este camino. Selva grita, "Paraíso se perdió"
Cucurrucú paloma. Dicen que yo perdí. Aunque estoy en el "otro
      lado", La Misma Luna brilla para tí
Se mira el mismo cielo lindo, desde enero hasta diciembre

96

Cuando miramos La Misma Luna,

       Astros del cielo se acuerdan siempre

The Story of Dolores

One day in the early morn, I heard an angel sing
It was a March on Washington led by Martin Luther King

I'd heard of Rosa Parks—they taught me about Montgomery
I even heard of, "Sí Se Puede," but I was shocked at a discovery

You can't erase us from history so we have to tell the story
About a social justice warrior. Time has come to shine in glory

April 10 is sacred. The day Zapata died
But April 10, 1930, there was a Rainbow in the sky

We all have a genesis, our stories have their birth
This little girl grew to woman who dares to change this earth

See, I'm California born and raised. My skin darkens in the sun
I'm from the Inland Empire, but I thought I was the only one

They told me those with skin of bronze couldn't make it to the top
They told me not to dream so big. Tried to make our vision stop

They said that girls should stay behind. Go to the back seat of
    the bus and take it
They even said that boys like me were too nice. I'd never make it

I wanted to be like Superman. I had dreams of going far
But I thought I was alone, so I looked for a shining star

Searching high and searching low, I asked for God to send

God send me a superhero, or just send me a friend

See the nights were cold and lonely, and I was small and meek
I looked for someone who looked like me, was this so much to seek?

This morning I listened to the sound. Zenzontle, the mockingbird
When the caged bird sings of freedom   Songs of Freedom
        must be heard

"Tiahui" is the word the Mexica often say
Go Onward sons and daughters in that peaceful warrior way

        El son del movimiento   the song of De Colores
        Today we sing that song   The Story of Dolores...

Dicen

Dicen que estos ojos son ojos Indios. Dicen por ahí
Dicen que 'ste cabello es pelo negro, como el cuervo. Dicen por ahí
Me dicen que soy moreno. Soy el negrito en el verano
Y dicen que mi nariz es nariz de Azteca y que mi frente es Mexicano
Yo soy, yo soy Ramirez de Ríos y Arroyos de Tepehuán
Unidos en Toibingna con las estrellas, a recordar
Yo soy rey de los Reyes, rey de sirvientes. El servidor
Historia que destruyeron es recordado. Empieza el temblor
La Niña, La Pinta, La Santa Maria. Dios y Oro y Resplandor
Dicen que cruzamos fronteras. Dice mi Abuelo que no cruzamos
Venimos antes, desde el norte. Indígenas americanos
Dicen soy piel morena, mi piel de bronce de las fronteras
Yo vengo de Pomona, de California. Sagradas tierras
Donde crecía el encino; hoy, selvas de concreto—ríos se acabaron
Bulevar de Cahuenga; el sauz se fué—sueños quebraron
Sierra de Durango. Huracán de Culiacán
San Luis, Río Colorado. Morongo. Yuhaviatam
Somos, Somos La Gente. Únete Pueblo. Pueblo Odam
Cuando el Pueblo sea Unido. Tu corazón encontrarás
Tiahui, Parientes Nahuatl. Hacia adelante con dignidad
Hopi da luz a profecía. Como el que se está muriendo hay que rezar
Yo digo, "Soy ser humano." Sangre mestiza. Rojo, yo sangro
Colores del arcoiris. Soy otro Tú. Dime tu hermano
Fronteras que no cruzamos. Entre culturas—la soledad
Me dicen que me regrese.
     Dice Abuelito:
          Es Nuestro Hogar

They Say

They say these eyes are Indios. Eyes of the Indian. That's what they say
They tell me that my hair is black. Black like the crow that flies by day
They tell me I'm the darker one, that I'm el negro of Cumbia sounds
They say my nose is an Aztec one, and that on my forehead is El Nopal
I am, I am Ramirez from the Arroyos of Tepehuán
I am king of the Reyes, servant of servants. The king of kings
        Servant, I am
Hist'ry that's been erased. We shall bring it forward. Earth starts
        to tremble
Together we form a circle. The Kizh, Ohlone... The stars remember
Niña, Pinta, Santa Maria—god and Gold in all its Splendor
They say we crossed the border that crossed our people,
        Grandfather says
We came from the north before the Pueblo of Los Angeles
They say I'm piel morena with skin of bronze. From borderlands
I come to you from Pomona, from California. From Sacred Land
Where there were mighty Oak trees are concrete jungles instead
        of streams
Boulevard of Cahuenga. Instead of willows are broken dreams
Sierra of Durango. Hurricane of Culiacán.
San Luis, Rio Colorado. Morongo. Yuhaviatam
We are—We are The People. We are Odami from O'dam land
The People Shall Be United. Never defeated. Unite the People,
        pueblo Odam
Tiahui, Aho', our Nahuatl. Upward and Onward With Dignity
Hopi Wise One Prays like the Dying, Giving Birth to Prophecy
I say, "I am human." Blood of mestizo. My blood bleeds red

We sing "De Colores". Call me the Rainbow. Just Go Ahead
Borders that doubled-crossed us. Between the cultures. Am I alone?
They say, "Go back to your land"
    My Grandpa tells me
        This is our Home

Write our Legacy

I can hear the Mockingbird—the sound of the Zenzontle
Nature has wondrous music. Last night I heard Coyote
My brother's great lesson to me: "Go onward, sons and daughters"
Tiahui is the term to reach the cool fresh waters
We light the sage as the Mexica light up the copal
And in the smoke the vision's clear, Águila y nopal
For the blood lines flow so deep, time immemorial
The Scrub Jay's had so much to teach, so has the Oriole
The lessons surely multiply growing wisdom so great
Teach us about destiny to co-create our fate
Now everything is different since that fateful day
Atomic bombs we have created. Now we must H.A.L.T. and pray
Prayer without action never works, we're told
Must be backed with energy, and action must be **BOLD**
We live in uncertain times. This is the eleventh hour
That fateful moment has arrived. Time is now to act with power
The greatest power is ahimsa. It surely isn't force
We act with love and never violence—lead the planet on the
      right course
We are the stewards. Protect our planet! Cherish Mother Earth
If we don't heed the omen, we lose reason for our birth
And as we heed the messages we will not just survive
We practice Satyagraha. We unite and thrive
The Condor and the Eagle join, fulfilling Prophecy
      You Must Write the Chapter to continue OUR LEGACY

IX

The Last Section: The Beginning

New Beginning

I was a child in Pomona. A youngster with a dream.
We traveled through Ganesha Hills. We walked along the stream.
Like the People of the Willow, underneath those red-tailed hawks.
Woke up by a lake called Puddingstone, to songs of the meadowlarks.
The Kizh, Odam, Yuhaviatam—the lessons we'd learn later—
O'odham is for Our People—who still live out, "Love thy Neighbor."
It's "We" for "We the People". David and I, best friends.
We traveled in a trio with our protector to the end.
We spent nights beneath the great horned owl, as coyotes lurked
        in packs.
Our triangle was one of courage. In those nights, fear we lacked.
Our protector was our dog named Dino—for a dog's a boy's
        best friend.
I believe he's shining down on us, as he was loyal to the end.
...And We means that We Can. I cannot do this alone.
Together we learned lessons as we walked to Puddingstone.
"If you want fair go to Pomona," as the old-timers would say.
We must have been the lucky ones, 'cause the fair was along the way.
But my life sure ain't no fairy tale, as my dreams turned to dust.
My life burned down to ashes and was corroded to rust.
I chased castles in the sky. I built with no foundation.
Searching to fill a broken heart, I fell into temptation.
Double lives and secrecy, I bowed my head in shame.
But I still shocked you with my arrogance. I saw you and placed
        the blame.
Nothing could fill my cup or quench my thirst for more.
So instead of chasing broken dreams, I walk right through that door.

So I'm back at the beginning, on Berkeley Avenue.

Where those parrots descended from the sky. Where those
persimmons grew.

I'm here in Pomona, right where I started from.

Where Berkeley meets those sycamores, where I have lost and won.

This building is a triangle like pyramids of old.

Unity, service, recovery. Our stories must be told.

Experience, strength, and hope. I hear you testify.

You'll experience new freedom. Like that mighty hawk, you'll fly.

I celebrate a milestone. We share. We laugh. We pray.

But the old timers remind us. We only have today.

Sometimes I feel I've lost. Sometimes I feel I'm winning.

We do this one day at a time.

This is our new Beginning

Tariq: the Morning Star

When I was young, my Mama taught me, "To be good is to forgive."
When you have love deep in your heart, this love is yours to give.
I was taught about a savior who practiced love and peace.
They led me by example. Told me, "Love contains the keys."
Now I'm older and experienced, and I search for peace within.
I must admit I can get angry with strangers as with kin.
I traveled high and low, searching for Solutions.
Trying to teach about forgiveness, as we hear vengeance
      and retribution.
Though I'm trying to practice love, I admit I've been a preacher.
When it comes down to forgiveness, I'd like to be student
      and teacher.
I met a man the other day. Azim Khamisa is his name.
I met him in Pomona, and I'm so glad he came.
He traveled from across the seas searching for a better life.
He set sail for America to leave violence and strife.
He married Almas. Had a child. Tariq, their only son.
But at the tender age of 20 he was the victim of a gun.
The family's heart was broken. Justice seemed just right.
"Lock the killer up for life. Prison all day and night."
The killer was a mere 14 years old. News traveled 'round the nation.
Azim prayed to God and God is great. Tony's also God's creation.
Azim met the family of Tony Hicks, the killer of his son.
Who's gonna stop this violent cycle? Azim said, "I'll be the one."
It's children killing children. The gangs of the USA.
It's gonna take more than preaching. It's not enough to pray.
Prayer must be met with action to create a better way.

And   We Shall Begin a   MOVEMENT. Perhaps you'll join today.

Tariq Khamisa lives through us. His legacy will shine.

For his father lives a simple rule: to forgive is divine.

We've seen violence from the start of time—since Abel was killed
>   by Cain.

But if we break this cycle, Tariq's death won't be in vain.

And now there's a foundation that bears the name Tariq.

It gives hope to the hopeless. Gives the Earth to the meek.

I write this in Pomona, where we're not immune to violence.

Let our actions speak louder than our words. Let's break all of
>   the silence.

For mightier than a bullet, more powerful than hatred's wrath.

Shalom, salam, paz, peace, ahimsa—I call it the Perfect Path.

See, Pomona's Reawakening! There's so much work to do.

Creating Compassionate Communities. With compassion we'll
>   start anew.

Tariq's legacy of love lives on, from Pomona to afar.

They say he died in San Diego, but Tariq's now a shining star.

Above the desert is the Morning Star. La Estrella del Amanecer.

Like the stars above Pomona. Just like Mama said.

See, **it's time to heal the World today**, for Tariq has touched
>   our hearts.

We thought we saw the end of a life, but what we see is

>   **the Very Start.**

Bring Heaven Back to Earth

Broken. But not to my core.

All filled up, but keep askin' for more.

Insatiable. Like an addiction.

Can't find the cure for this affliction.

Restless. And discontent.

"S.O.S." is the message I've sent.

Witch doctors. I need some healing.

Desperately. Didn't think I'd be kneeling.

Father please forgive me for I know not what I've done.

I've waited for a sign as clear as the rising sun.

Paralyzed. Will you answer me?

Hypnotized. By my legacy.

Lost in my own fantasy, I began to believe my press.

Even had apostles. Wanted stardom, nothing less.

Soaring through the galaxy. Won't meet another of my type.

So high in the stratosphere, I got lost in my own hype.

Millionaire to billionaire.

Public at large all stopped to stare.

Invented my own style. Don't need Armani or Versace.

Paparazzi love fake smiles when the whole world is watching.

Don't buckle under pressure. You've got too much at stake.

Watch out when you're at the pinnacle. If you're not careful you
        might break.

Woke up to an omen. Gotta turn my fate around.

Thought I was invincible. My world came tumbling down.

They may say it's rock bottom. There's only one way to go. That's up.

Thought they were friends. They backstab. As I ask, "What the fuq?'

Lesson learned as I got burned. It was all of my making.

Grandiose. Thought I'd arrived. I may have mastered taking.

Now I taste humility. A hard life that I'm living.

There's a message in that adage: We do receive from giving.

Hard work, I find. A different kind. I've sweat as I have toiled.

Character is built as I stand on different soil.

Reminiscent of my youth, from boredom I recoil.

Learning it the hard way as my blood begins to boil.

Said I was "Apocalypse".

Mighty bullets from my lips.

Now I find the answer to my malady.

Messiah isn't just in me. Savior is in community.

The beauty and the wonder; rhyme and rhythm of the verse.

Like Aurora Borealis belongs to the universe.

Saved. Down to my core.

Shall strive. Though I don't need more.

Found the answers to addiction.

Humble Love in Action. Healer of this grave affliction.

Was blind. Now I start to see.

Be kind. To the least of thee.

Won't have a one-man revolution.

In people power lies the solution.

We learn to gain some peace. As Gandhi learned from Jesus.

The wise man starts to speak. The curandera healed us.

Was a poor excuse. Many called me tragic.

Now I see you. I see magic.

One love, ahimsa, satyagraha—universal laws.

Thy kingdom come; thy will be done through peace, the greatest
cause.

Had lied to myself about paradise. Made a lot of money.

But Heaven now is mom's papitas, served with milk and honey.

Now the question comes: "What is Heaven to you?"
For me Heaven is a place where I can share my love with all of you.
I finally found a purpose—the reason for my birth.
And as we learn to dance, we'll bring Heaven Back to Earth.
Thought my world was over. My heart and soul were spinning.
Realize this is not the end:

This is a
BRIGHT BEGINNING.

Start Another Way

Unite The PEACEPROPHECIES

The Beginning's Here!

About the Author

Raised in a Mexican Roman Catholic family in Pomona, California, the young, nature-loving Gustavo Reyes Ramirez dreamed of one day becoming an author. He struggled with his sexual and cultural identities and succumbed to peer pressure as an adolescent, getting lost in a world of alcohol and other substances. His life changed as he began writing and empowering youth, and he graduated from UC Berkeley in Social Justice. He started an organization called *Access to Power*, utilizing language to inspire youth to achieve their dreams and live their purpose. Mr. Ramirez became a teacher and manifested many of his dreams, including being a television spokesperson and activist for progressive causes. He switched professions briefly to the Hollywood television industry as he fell to drugs—harder than ever before. Being diagnosed with mental illness, a psychiatrist's brutal words became a self-fulfilling prophecy of agony and broken dreams before Gustavo rekindled his creativity through poetry. This writing became a therapeutic outlet, as well as a way to turn suffering into beauty. Join Gustavo as he shares his life and inspires us all to enjoy beauty and miracles as we dare to bring peace to our communities and change the world.

DSTL
arts

This publication was produced by DSTL Arts.

DSTL Arts is a nonprofit arts mentorship organization that inspires, teaches, and hires emerging artists from underserved communities.

To learn more about DSTL Arts, visit online at:
DSTLArts.org
@DSTLArts

www.ingramcontent.com/pod-product-compliance
Lightning Source LLC
Chambersburg PA
CBHW060601100426
42744CB00008B/1263